WELCOME TO MY COUNTRY

Welcome to
SOUTH AFRICA

Gareth Stevens Publishing
A WORLD ALMANAC EDUCATION GROUP COMPANY

Written by
UMAIMA MULLA-FEROZE/MARY-ANN STOTKO

Edited in USA by
DOROTHY L. GIBBS

Designed by
GEOSLYN LIM

Picture research by
SUSAN JANE MANUEL

First published in North America in 2003 by
Gareth Stevens Publishing
A World Almanac Education Group Company
330 West Olive Street, Suite 100
Milwaukee, Wisconsin 53212 USA

Please visit our web site at:
www.garethstevens.com
For a free color catalog describing
Gareth Stevens' list of high-quality
books and multimedia programs,
call 1-800-542-2595 (USA) or
1-800-387-3178 (CANADA).
Gareth Stevens Publishing's fax: (414) 332-3567.

© **TIMES MEDIA PRIVATE LIMITED 2003**
Originated and designed by
Times Editions
An imprint of Times Media Private Limited
A member of the Times Publishing Group
Times Centre, 1 New Industrial Road
Singapore 536196
http://www.timesone.com.sg/te

Library of Congress Cataloging-in-Publication Data
Mulla-Feroze, Umaima.
Welcome to South Africa/ Umaima Mulla-Feroze and Mary-Ann Stotko.
p. cm. — (Welcome to my country)
Summary: An introduction to the geography, history, government, economy, people, and culture of South Africa.
Includes bibliographical references and index.
ISBN 0-8368-2547-0 (lib. bdg.)
1. South Africa—Juvenile literature. [1. South Africa.]
I. Stotko, Mary-Ann. II. Title. III. Series.
DT1719.M85   2003
968—dc21   2002030276

Printed in Malaysia

1 2 3 4 5 6 7 8 9 07 06 05 04 03

PICTURE CREDITS
Allsport/Mike Powell: 37 (bottom)
A.N.A. Press Agency: 5, 9 (top), 36
Andes Press Agency: 14 (bottom), 23, 24
Art Directors and Trip Photo Library: 16, 21,
    27, 31, 33 (bottom), 37 (top), 41 (top)
Bes Stock: 6, 32, 35, 43
Camera Press: 4, 8
Alain Evrard: cover, 20, 30, 45
Getty Images/HultonArchive: 12, 14 (top),
    15 (top), 15 (bottom)
Hans Hayden: 2, 7 (bottom), 9 (bottom)
The Hutchison Library: 19, 22, 25, 40,
    41 (bottom)
iAfrika: 13, 15 (center), 28
Images of Africa Photobank: 3 (bottom)
Imapress: 29 (left)
Jason Lauré: 1, 18, 38, 39 (top)
Liaison Agency: 17
North Wind Picture Archives: 10, 11
Christine Osborne Pictures: 26, 33 (top)
Mary-Ann Stotko: 44
Topham Picturepoint: 3 (top), 3 (center),
    7 (top), 29 (right), 34, 39 (bottom)

Digital Scanning by Superskill Graphics Pte Ltd

Contents

Words that appear in the glossary are printed in **boldface** type the first time they occur in the text.

Welcome to South Africa!

South Africa is a land of great variety. Besides having many kinds of plants, animals, and minerals, different regions of the country have different climates, and its people belong to many **ethnic groups**. Let's learn about the people and history of this "Rainbow Nation."

Opposite:
The Victoria and Albert waterfront is in Cape Town, one of South Africa's largest cities.

Below:
Today's young South Africans can look forward to a society of equality and justice.

The Flag of South Africa

South Africa adopted its current flag in 1994. The flag's six colors are a combination of the main colors in several earlier South African flags. The green section represents "unity in **diversity**," which is the nation's **motto**.

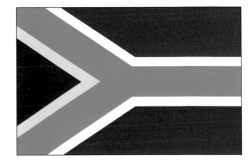

The Land

The Republic of South Africa is at the southern tip of the African continent, covering an area of 471,008 square miles (1,219,912 square kilometers). From west to east, the country shares its northern border with Namibia, Botswana, Zimbabwe, Mozambique, and Swaziland. The Indian Ocean is off South Africa's southeastern coast. The Atlantic Ocean is off its southwestern coast. The independent state of Lesotho lies within the borders of the South African republic.

Below:
The province of KwaZulu Natal has fertile plains that stretch from the southeastern coast to the Drakensberg Mountains.

Left: Mossel Bay, which is on the Indian Ocean in the province of Western Cape, is famous for its white beaches and spectacular views.

South Africa has deserts, beaches, grasslands, **subtropics**, and mountains. The Kalahari Desert is a big part of its northwestern region, and a long, mountainous **ridge**, called the Great Escarpment, separates the country's coastal areas from its inner **plateau**.

Rising 11,182 feet (3,408 meters), Mount Njesuthi is South Africa's highest peak. Flowing 1,300 miles (2,092 kilometers), the Orange River is the longest, but the Vaal and the Limpopo are also major rivers.

Below: The Indian and Atlantic Oceans meet at the Cape of Good Hope, South Africa's southernmost point. The Cape of Good Hope is known for its stormy weather, rough seas, and dangerous rocks and reefs.

Climate

Most of South Africa has a temperate climate, with mild weather and warm temperatures, but the country's western coast is usually cool and dry, while the eastern coast is hot and **humid**. Located in the southern hemisphere, South Africa's seasons are always just the opposite of those in the northern hemisphere. Summer, then, is from December through February. Winter is from June through August.

Above: In South Africa's mild and sunny climate, wildflowers bloom all year round.

Plants and Animals

Plant life varies from one region to another in South Africa, ranging from desert plants to evergreen forests and including about twenty thousand kinds of flowers. An abundance of wildlife includes monkeys and mongooses as well as jackals, ostriches, and many other species of cats and birds. With over a hundred kinds of snakes, South Africa also has its share of reptiles.

Above: South Africa's rhinoceroses are part of a group of mammals nicknamed the "Big Five." Other animals in this group are lions, leopards, buffalo, and elephants.

Left: The king protea is a rare and unusual looking flower. Found only in South Africa, it is the country's national flower.

History

The San were the first people known to live in South Africa. By A.D. 100, other groups, including the Khoikhoi and Bantu-speaking tribes from central Africa, had joined the San. By 1500, the Nguni people had settled along the eastern coast.

European Settlers

In 1652, the Dutch established Cape Colony, the first European settlement in South Africa. Over many decades,

Left: The **Dutch East India Company** was involved in founding Cape Colony. It was a stopping place for trading ships sailing between Rotterdam and the Far East.

Left:
This illustration shows a nineteenth-century farm in Orange Free State. The discovery of diamonds in Orange Free State and gold in Transvaal drew more British settlers to South Africa.

French and German settlers joined the Dutch at Cape Colony. The Europeans became known as the *Boers* (BOO-ers).

In 1814, Cape Colony was given to the British. Many Boers were against British rule and moved further inland. Some settled in Natal, (now KwaZulu Natal). Others moved north, across the Orange and the Vaal Rivers, forming the new Boer republics of Orange Free State (now Free State) and Transvaal, in the early 1850s.

In 1910, after the arrival of many more British settlers, the Boer republics joined the British colonies to form the Union of South Africa.

The Beginning of Apartheid

Under the Union's **constitution**, only the white people of South Africa could hold positions of power. Led by Louis Botha, the South African Party (SAP) government promoted *apartheid* (ah-PAHRT-hate), which separated white and nonwhite South Africans in every possible way. To oppose apartheid, black leaders formed the South African Native National Congress, later called the African National Congress (ANC).

Left: In the 1950s, only white children could play in this pond at Pretoria National Botanical Gardens. Signs on everything from park benches to buses identified who was allowed to use them.

Years of Apartheid

In 1914, General James Barry Hertzog,
a former SAP member, founded the
National Party. When this party came
to power in 1948, it strengthened the
apartheid policy. Between the 1950s
and the 1970s black South Africans led
strong protests against the government,
and more of them joined the ANC, then
led by Nelson Mandela. Police brutally
punished protestors, many of whom
died in their fight for equality.

Becoming a Democracy

By the 1980s, the economy of South Africa was suffering because many countries would not trade with South Africa as long as it upheld apartheid. Although the government made some **reforms**, they were not enough to satisfy the country's black population.

In 1989, President F. W. de Klerk introduced reforms toward establishing a **democracy**, and apartheid laws were slowly lifted. The ANC won the first democratic elections, in 1994, and Nelson Mandela became president.

Above: Nelson Mandela is a symbol of South Africa's fight for freedom. He was jailed for twenty-seven years for his role in the antigovernment protests of the 1960s. Mandela was released from prison in 1990.

Left: On May 10, 1994, many black South Africans gathered in the country's capital, Pretoria, to watch Nelson Mandela become the first black president of South Africa.

Christiaan Neethling Barnard (1922–2001)

Cape Town surgeon Dr. Christiaan Barnard performed the first human heart transplant, in 1967, and received the first World Health Award, in 2000.

Christiaan Neethling Barnard

Zensi Miriam Makeba (1932–)

In the 1950s, Zensi Miriam Makeba was a famous black South African singer. In 1960, because of her anti-apartheid views, her songs were banned, and she was forced into **exile**. She returned to South Africa in 1990.

Zensi Miriam Makeba

Desmond Mpilo Tutu (1931–)

Winner of the 1984 Nobel Prize for Peace, Desmond Tutu strongly criticized apartheid and supported nonviolent protests for equal rights. From 1986 to 1996, he was the archbishop of Cape Town and head of South Africa's Anglican Church.

Desmond Mpilo Tutu

Government and the Economy

South Africa has three branches of government. The legislative branch, or Parliament, consists of a National Assembly, with 350 to 400 members, and the National Council of Provinces, which has 90 members. All members of Parliament are elected by the people.

The president and a **cabinet** of advisors form the executive branch. The National Assembly elects one of its members to become president.

Left:
South Africa's main Parliament building is in Cape Town. Constructed in 1885, it has been used for legislative purposes since the Union of South Africa was formed, in 1910.

Left: Thabo Mbeki became South Africa's second black president on June 16, 1999.

Then the president chooses Assembly members to serve on the cabinet and to head government departments.

The government's judicial branch includes all of South Africa's courts. The highest is the Constitutional Court. The country also has a Supreme Court of Appeals and a number of high courts and local courts.

Economy

Since the discovery of diamonds in 1867 and gold in 1886, mining has been South Africa's most important industry. The country produces more gem diamonds than any other nation in the world. Large reserves of other minerals and metals, including coal, iron ore, copper, nickel, manganese, and uranium, are also important to the South African economy.

Below: Bounded by the Atlantic and Indian Oceans, South Africa has plenty of seafood, including mackerel, herring, anchovies, and rock lobsters.

Left: This South African miner is working at a gold mine in Gauteng. Over one hundred years of mining has not exhausted the nation's gold resources.

Manufacturing and Agriculture

Metal products, especially iron and steel, are a big part of South Africa's manufacturing industry. Most of the nation's industrial activity is in Gauteng and the cities of Cape Town, Durban, and Port Elizabeth. Other manufactured products include food and beverages, chemicals, and **textiles**.

Only 12 percent of South Africa's land is used for agriculture. The main crops are wheat, corn, potatoes, grapes, sugarcane, peanuts, and tobacco.

People and Lifestyle

Multicultural South Africa has four main racial groups. About 75 percent of the people are blacks. Most of them live in the countryside. The rest of the people usually identify themselves as whites, coloreds, or Indians. Most of the people in these groups live in cities.

About 14 percent of South Africans are considered whites. The majority, called Afrikaners, are descendants of the Boers. The other whites are called English-speakers.

Left: In today's democratic South Africa, people of all races can be friends. Before 1991, apartheid laws kept South Africans of different races strictly separated.

Left: Not all of South Africa's black population speak the same language. The nation's blacks have four different language groups: Nguni, Sotho-Tswana, Tsonga, and Venda.

Coloreds, about 9 percent of the population, have mixed roots, sharing European, Malay, and native African ancestry. Many live in Cape Town.

Less than 3 percent of the people are Indians whose ancestors were workers brought to South Africa's sugar plantations in the mid-1800s.

Left: Houses like this one in KwaZulu Natal have no running water or electricity. The South Africans who live in these houses are usually poor blacks.

From Homelands to Shantytowns

Many of South Africa's blacks live in areas once called homelands. These areas are found only in the countryside. Homeland families are usually large, and children often starve because their parents cannot find work. They have no money for food, and the soil is too poor to grow enough food.

To take care of their families, many South Africans have been moving to the cities in search of work. The flow of people coming from the countryside has created housing shortages in South

African cities, so **shantytowns** have grown around them. Many homeless South Africans are living in makeshift houses built with scraps of wood, iron, and cardboard.

Most whites, wealthy coloreds and Indians, and a small number of blacks enjoy a high standard of living in South African cities and **suburbs**. Most have small families and beautiful homes but have to deal with a high rate of crime.

Below: The houses of wealthy families, such as this one in Johannesburg, often have tennis courts, swimming pools, and large gardens.

Education

Under apartheid law, students of different racial groups had to attend separate schools, and the different schools did not all offer the same quality of education.

Today, the country's democratic government is working hard to create a nonracial system with the same quality of education for all South Africans.

Below:
The government of South Africa has a target goal to have no less than one teacher for every forty students in each school. To achieve this goal, many black students now go to schools in areas that are mainly white.

From ages seven through fifteen, all South African children must attend school. Elementary school lasts six years and has two levels: a junior level (grades one through three) and a senior level (grades four through six). High school also lasts six years and has two levels. After grade nine, students can either leave school or go on to senior high. At the end of grade twelve, they take an examination to earn a Senior Certificate. With good grades on the certificate, they can enter a university.

Left: South Africa has three Dutch Reformed churches. With four million members, the Dutch Reformed Church in Western Cape *(left)* has the largest following.

Religion

Before the European settlers brought Christianity to South Africa in the 1600s, the native peoples had their own religions. All traditional African religions believed in a supreme being and worshiped spirits with the power to affect people's daily lives. Today, about 28 percent of South Africans still practice the traditional religions.

About two-thirds of the population, however, are Christians. More than four million South Africans, including most of the country's Afrikaners, about half of the coloreds, and a few blacks, belong to the Dutch Reformed Church. Many blacks and most white English-speakers are Anglicans, Methodists, or Roman Catholics. The rest of the South African people are mostly Muslims, Hindus, or Jews.

Below:
These worshipers are attending a service at a Zionist church in Durban. With about two million followers, the Zion Christian Church is the largest in a new branch of Christian faiths combining Western religious practices with those of traditional African religions.

Language

English is one of South Africa's eleven official languages. The other ten are Afrikaans and nine Bantu languages: Ndebele, Pedi, Sotho, Swazi, Tsonga, Tswana, Venda, Xhosa, and Zulu.

English is spoken mainly by South Africa's Indians and English-speakers. Most Afrikaners and many coloreds speak Afrikaans, which came from the Dutch language spoken by settlers in the 1600s. Most blacks speak Zulu.

Left:
The selection of magazines at this newsstand in Cape Town includes both local and foreign publications.

Left:
Nadine Gordimer (1923–) (*far left*), a white South African novelist and short-story writer, won the Nobel Prize for Literature in 1991. Alan Paton (1903–1988) (*left*) is best known for his novel *Cry the Beloved Country*, one of the most famous books written during apartheid.

Literature

South African literature includes works written in the English, Afrikaans, and Bantu languages. The country's first English book, *The Story of an African Farm*, was written by Olive Schreiner (1855–1920) in 1883. Well-known Afrikaners André Brink (1935–) and Breyten Breytenbach (1939–) wrote openly against apartheid. Breytenbach was even forced into exile. The works of Thomas Mofolo (1876–1948) are in Sotho. B. W. Vilakazi (1905–1947) is famous for his Zulu poems.

Arts

Painting

As far back as the Stone Age, the San people were painting scenes of family life, hunting, and fighting on the rock walls of caves all over South Africa. Landscape painter J. E. A. Volschenk (1853–1936), however, is considered the country's first professional artist. Anton van Wouw (1862–1945) is one of South Africa's best known sculptors.

Below: Murals, or wall paintings, are a traditional art form of black South Africans, especially the Ndebele tribe, who decorate their homes with bright colors and bold patterns.

Music

Music is an important part of South African life, especially in tribal rituals and ceremonies. Traditional African tribal music is sung or played on drums or other instruments, such as animal horns and xylophones. A popular kind of Zulu tribal music called *iscathamiya* (is-COT-ah-me-yah) is sung without accompanying instruments. *Mbaqanga* (um-bah-TZAN-gah) is a popular kind of dance music started by the blacks.

Architecture

For centuries, native African tribes have built many styles of mud and grass huts. Today, the beehive-shaped *kraals* (KRAHLS) of the Zulus are the most widely recognized.

Western Cape's Cape Dutch-style buildings, of the 1600s and 1700s, are probably the most **distinctive** South African architecture. In the 1800s, the British **revived** styles such as **Gothic**.

Above: The Groot Constantia in Cape Town is an example of seventeenth-century Cape Dutch architecture. Built around 1685, it is the oldest building in Western Cape.

Dance

From tribal to modern, South Africa's distinctive dance styles reflect both the nation's history and its ethnic cultures. *Toyi-toyi* (TOY-TOY), for example, combines protest-style marching from the apartheid years and traditional Zulu dance steps.

While many tribal groups have their own special dance styles, classical ballet is also popular in South Africa. Professional ballet companies perform in both Pretoria and Cape Town.

Above:
The beautiful bead-work made by Zulu women is admired around the world. A story is woven into every piece, using a secret code of colors that only Zulus understand.

Left: Traditional handicrafts made in South Africa include handwoven baskets and carved wooden masks. They are sold in city marketplaces as well as along the roads between cities and large towns.

Leisure

South Africans who live in or near cities enjoy a wide variety of leisure activities. They can go to movies, live theater performances, museums, and art galleries. They can visit with friends at restaurants, tea gardens, or coffee shops. Just a short drive takes them to nearby parks and nature reserves for hiking and other outdoor activities.

Below: Children in rural areas of South Africa often turn old tin cans, bottle tops, and other discarded objects into toys. These young boys in Eastern Cape are having a lot of fun with two old tires.

Left: People who live near Hout Bay, in Western Cape, can spend some of their leisure time at the beach. South Africa's 1,739-mile (2,798-km) coastline means plenty of swimming and sunbathing.

South Africans who live in rural areas must work long hours to earn a living. Many are farmers. Some make and sell handicrafts. Because they do not have much leisure time, they try to build their social lives into their workdays. Many women work together, at either daily chores, such as washing and cooking; or crafts, such as beadwork, **embroidery**, and basket making, so they can chat and exchange news.

Sports

Whether playing or watching, South Africans love sports. Before 1992, however, South African athletes were banned from competing internationally. Many countries refused to play against South African teams because of the country's apartheid laws.

The children of South Africa have a wide range of sports available to them. Boys and girls participate in volleyball, hockey, tennis, swimming, and track and field. Boys also play soccer, rugby, and cricket.

Below:
South Africa has more than thirty thousand soccer clubs, with training facilities for over a million players. Most players on the country's soccer teams are black.

Soccer is, by far, the favorite sport of black South Africans. In June 2001, South Africa's national soccer team, Bafana Bafana, was ranked twenty-fourth in the world.

Track and field events are also very popular in South Africa. The country has produced several world-class, long-distance runners, including Hendrick Ramaala, Lucas Matlala, and Colin Thomas. South Africa's very difficult 54-mile (87-km) Comrades Marathon, held every June, is an internationally known running event.

Below: Competing in the marathon at the 1996 Olympics in Atlanta, Georgia, Josia Thugwane became the first black South African to win an Olympic gold medal.

National Holidays

The 1996 constitution passed by the democratic South African government removed all apartheid-related holidays from the country's calendar. Today, the national holidays in South Africa are Human Rights' Day (March 21), Freedom Day (April 27), Youth Day (June 16), National Women's Day (August 9), and Day of Reconciliation (December 16). Good Friday (March or April) and Christmas (December 25) are also considered national holidays.

Traditional Festivals

South Africa's black tribal groups have many traditional festivals that celebrate major life events. Initiation, when a child becomes an adult, is one of the most important. Initiation for a Xhosa boy means leaving his village for a time, shaving his head, and smearing white clay all over his body. When he returns, he is covered with red clay for three months. After that, he is a man.

Above:
A white blanket with red bands is special clothing for a Xhosa initiation.

Left:
Every year, in September, Zulus celebrate Shaka's Day. On Shaka's Day, Zulus wear traditional clothing and do ritual dances at Shaka's tomb in KwaZulu Natal. Shaka was the founder of the Zulu kingdom.

Food

Traditional African food is very simple. Cornmeal porridge, called *pap* (PUP), is the main food at almost every meal. Pap is eaten with milk for breakfast. For lunch or dinner, it is served with a sauce or in a vegetable stew with meat.

Waterblommetjie bredie (VAH-ter-bloh-mer-key BREAR-dee), made with waterlilies that grow only in Western Cape, is a unique South African dish.

Opposite:
For many black South Africans, pap served with a tomato-based gravy is a popular lunchtime meal.

Below:
These children in Soweto are eating their pap with vegetables.

Dishes influenced by Malay **cuisine** include sweet curries and *bobotie* (ber-BOW-ah-tee), which is minced beef or lamb baked with onions, lemons, curry powder, and **turmeric**. It is usually served with yellow rice.

Afrikaner meals generally include meats such as beef, lamb, and wild game and vegetables such as sweet potatoes or pumpkin. *Biltong* (bill-TONG) is a common Afrikaner snack. It is dried strips of meat that have been soaked in salt.

Below: Beginning after 1652, Dutch settlers were South Africa's first wine-makers. Today, the wineries in Western Cape make world-class products.

SOUTH AFRICA

Tropic of Capricorn

A B C D

1

BOTSWANA

NAMIBIA

2

K a l a h a r i

D e s e r t

NORTH-WEST

GAUTENG

■ **PRETOR**

Johannesburg

● **Soweto**

Vaal

N

Orange

3

FREE STATE

Mount Ntsuthi
(11,182 feet / 3,408 m)

NORTHERN CAPE

● **Bloemfontein**

LESOTHO

Orange

Drakens

EASTERN CAPE

4

WESTERN CAPE

ATLANTIC OCEAN

Hout Bay ● **Cape Town**

Mossel Bay

Cape of
Good Hope

● **Port Elizabeth**

INDIAN

OCEAN

5

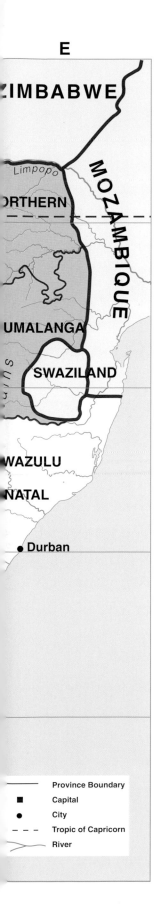

E

ZIMBABWE

Limpopo

MOZAMBIQUE

NORTHERN

UMALANGA

SWAZILAND

WAZULU

NATAL

• Durban

Province Boundary
■ Capital
● City
– – Tropic of Capricorn
〰 River

Above: Few South Africans live near the Drakensberg Mountains.

Atlantic Ocean
A3–A5

Bloemfontein C3
Botswana B1–D2

Cape of Good
Hope A5
Cape Town A5

Drakensberg
Mountains D4–E2
Durban E3

Eastern Cape
(province) C5–D4

Free State (province)
C4–D3

Gauteng
(province) D2
Great Escarpment
A3–D4

Hout Bay A5

Indian Ocean B5–E2

Johannesburg D2

Kalahari Desert
B2–C2
KwaZulu Natal
(province) D4–E3

Lesotho D3–D4
Limpopo River
D2–E1

Mossel Bay B5
Mount Njesuthi D3
Mozambique E1–E3
Mpumalanga
(province) D2–E3

Namibia A1–B3
North-West
(province) C2–D3

Northern (province)
D1–E2
Northern Cape
(province) A3–C4

Orange River A3–C4

Port Elizabeth C5
Pretoria D2

Soweto D2
Swaziland E2–E3

Vaal River C3–D2

Western Cape
(province) A4–C5

Zimbabwe D1–E1

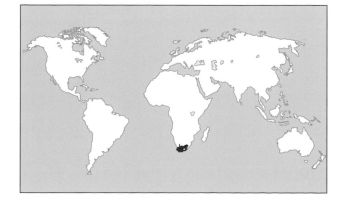

Quick Facts

Official Name	Republic of South Africa
Capital Cities	Pretoria (executive capital)
	Bloemfontein (judicial capital)
	Cape Town (legislative capital)
Official Languages	Afrikaans, English, Ndebele, Pedi, Sotho, Swazi, Tsonga, Tswana, Venda, Xhosa, Zulu
Population	43,647,658 (2002 estimate)
Land Area	471,008 square miles (1,219,912 square km)
Provinces	Eastern Cape, Free State, Gauteng, KwaZulu Natal, Mpumalanga, North-West, Northern, Nothern Cape, Western Cape
Highest Point	Mount Njesuthi 11,182 feet (3,408 m)
Major Rivers	Limpopo, Orange, Vaal
Major National Holidays	Human Rights' Day (March 21), Freedom Day (April 27), Youth Day (June 16), National Women's Day (August 9), Day of Reconciliation (December 16)
Currency	Rand (10.10 ZAR = U.S. $1 in 2002)

Opposite: This boy is standing on a hill that overlooks the coast of KwaZulu Natal.

Glossary

apartheid: a policy of separating racial groups so that nonwhites do not have equal political, economic, and social rights and advantages.

cabinet: a council of advisors that helps the leader of a country manage a government.

constitution: a document that contains the basic laws and principles of a nation.

cuisine: a specialized style of preparing and cooking foods.

democracy: a political system in which people rule themselves by electing representatives to make laws and run the government.

distinctive: having special qualities that make something stand out or seem different than others of its kind.

diversity: a state of having elements that are unlike one another.

Dutch East India Company: a major shipping business in the Netherlands that controlled most Dutch trade with the Far East in the 1600s and 1700s.

embroidery: the art of decorating fabric by hand-stitching colorful designs on it with a needle and thread.

ethnic groups: cultures of people who have the same heritage and customs.

exile: the state of being sent away by force from a person's native land.

Gothic: a richly decorated style of architecture popular in Western Europe in the Middle Ages.

humid: damp, usually describing the amount of moisture in the air.

motto: a saying or phrase that expresses a guiding principle.

plateau: a wide area of high, flat land.

reforms: changes made to correct faults or solve problems.

revived: brought back into use.

ridge: a long, narrow strip of raised land such as hills or mountains.

shantytowns: sections of cities where people live in crudely built shelters.

subtropics: the geographic areas closest to the hot, damp area near the equator.

suburbs: small communities located at the edges of larger towns or cities.

textiles: woven cloth or fabrics or products made of cloth or fabric.

turmeric: a powdery yellow spice with a strong taste and odor, from an East Indian plant related to ginger.